Original title:
Earthbound Epics

Copyright © 2025 Creative Arts Management OÜ
All rights reserved.

Author: Benjamin Caldwell
ISBN HARDBACK: 978-1-80566-685-1
ISBN PAPERBACK: 978-1-80566-970-8

Mystic Footprints in the Sand

On the beach where seagulls squawk,
A crab plays tag with a flip-flop rock.
Footprints dance in the sun's gleam,
Chasing shadows like a daydream.

Waves whisper tales of salty fries,
While sunbathers roar like lions in size.
A child builds castles with buckets of sand,
Only to find a dog has it planned.

The tide rolls in, a sneaky thief,
Swiping snacks without any grief.
A picnic spoiled by a crafty gull,
Who swoops in quick, oh what a pull!

Yet laughter rings from the ocean side,
As sun-kissed faces wear smiles wide.
Amidst the chaos, joy finds a way,
In this sandy circus, we play all day.

Chronicles of Intertwining Roots

Beneath the trees, the whispers weave,
As roots embrace, they schemingly cleave.
A squirrel's baby, taking aim,
Misses its mark, oh such a shame!

The old oak groans with every breeze,
While caterpillars munch on leaves with ease.
A meeting of mushrooms starts quite late,
Discussing plans to tango and mate.

Ants march proud in uniform lines,
Stealing crumbs like secretive spies.
But one lost bug ends up in a stew,
Outsmarted by a clever blue shoe.

The roots still twist and laugh aloud,
In their own world, merry and proud.
For in this dance beneath the ground,
Life's funny stories abound and resound.

Beneath the Canopy's Embrace

In a forest thick with tall trees,
Squirrels plot heists with great ease.
They stash nuts like hidden gold,
While birds sing tales, funny and bold.

The raccoons hold a moonlit feast,
Cheese and crackers, what a beast!
They dance in circles, sly and spry,
While owls hoot jokes from way up high.

Chronicles of Distant Horizons

The seashells gossip on the shore,
Telling tall tales of pirates' lore.
A crab in sunglasses struts with flair,
While seagulls plot schemes from the air.

Pelicans fly in coordinated styles,
As jellyfish dance with goofy smiles.
They swirl and twirl in watery play,
Creating chaos in their own way.

The Skyward Dance of Shadows

In the twilight's glow of fading light,
Shadows gather for a comedic night.
They trip and tumble, such a sight,
As laughter echoes, pure delight.

A shadow cat chases its own tail,
While a tree trunk tells a crazy tale.
Together they plot a silly prank,
Sneaking up on a dozing gank.

Beneath the Cerulean Skies

Under skies so vast and blue,
A flock of ducks wearing hats, who knew?
They quack in rhythm, strutting along,
Making nature their own song.

A turtle in shades slowly moves by,
While butterflies giggle, oh so sly.
Nature's circus, all in a row,
Bringing laughter wherever they go.

Reflections in the Still Waters

In the lake, a fish did grin,
Thinking all the world was in,
It twirled and splashed with all its might,
Even made the frogs take flight.

A duck quacked loud, 'What a show!'
While minnows danced beneath the flow,
The frog replied with quite a plop,
'We've never seen a fish do bop!'

The reeds swayed gently, laughed in breeze,
As turtles pondered with such ease,
The sun reflected on the waves,
'What a life for goofy knaves!'

With each ripple, a joke was cast,
In the stillness, a mighty blast,
The water sang in witty tones,
And life spoke back in funny moans.

Harmony of Earth and Sky

A bird once said, 'Look at me soar!'
While ants marched in a tiny chore,
Clouds just giggled, 'You think you're grand?'
'We hide the sun, but don't lend a hand!'

The mountains chuckled, 'Let's play a game,'
'Climb us, and we'll grant you fame!'
But little ants, they never tried,
They just looked up and wondered why.

The rivers whispered, 'Flow this way!'
While rocks sat still, enjoying the play,
The wind swooped down, a goofy tease,
'Catch me if you can, if you please!'

And nature laughed in vibrant hues,
In this symphony of playful views,
From earth beneath to skies above,
The dance of life was full of love.

In the Sanctuary of Stone

In caves so dark, the critters creep,
In search of snacks before they sleep,
A mouse in slippers squeaked with cheer,
'Who knew the rocks would be our pier?'

The stalactites dripped, a slow reprise,
Giving echoes to the mice's cries,
While bats just hung in silly style,
Dreaming of flight just for a while.

When moles gathered in secret huddle,
They debated why the ground was muddle,
They shouted, 'It's so plain to see!'
'We dig through dirt for glee and glee!'

In every crevice, laughter rings,
As nature hums with silly flings,
A sanctuary full of fun,
Where stone and critters come undone.

Tides of Memory on the Shore

Along the beach, the crabs did dance,
With little shuffles, in a trance,
The waves just winked and rolled in glee,
'Come join us, watch our jubilee!'

A seagull squawked, 'I know a joke!'
While turtles laughed and started to poke,
'When tides come in, we can all surf!'
And that's how crabs found their turf.

But jellyfish floated, quite aloof,
Saying, 'We're the true goof-proof!'
As shells debated which one to wear,
Fashioned by sand, unaware of despair.

And as the ocean sang its song,
Everyone joined, where they belong,
In the tides of life upon the shore,
Each memory waved for fun once more.

The Legacy of Forgotten Peaks

Once upon a summit high,
Llamas danced beneath the sky.
They wore tutus, what a sight!
Snowball fights in sheer delight.

Yet legends say, as stories go,
One llama stole the show!
He rapped and spun with pure finesse,
While others tried to impress, no less.

Now every peak holds laughter's sound,
Where every laugh has joy unbound.
Echoes ring from every height,
Of llamas prancing day and night.

A legacy wrapped in shear glee,
Reminding us to dance carefree.
So if you trek through hilly lanes,
Beware of llamas with grand plans!

The Breath of Worldly Wandering

Wandering whimsies on the trail,
A snail once dreamed of a grand sale.
With its shell as a fancy booth,
Selling wisdom and the truth.

A hedge maze met a wandering muse,
Who got lost and started to snooze.
Awoke to find a chicken's choir,
Singing tunes that never tire.

Frogs in jackets played the lute,
While crickets danced in fancy suit.
The world a stage, absurd and bright,
Where nonsense blooms day and night.

So if you find your feet do roam,
In joys of jest, you'll find your home.
A breath of laughter, wild and free,
A silly life, just wait and see!

A Symphony of Lost Seasons

In winter's grasp, the snowmen sigh,
They long to make their spirits fly.
But hats keep falling in the snow,
A slippery way to say hello.

Spring rolls in with sneaky pranks,
As bunnies hop in flower tanks.
They hide the eggs in bushes wide,
While children giggle and abide.

Summer brings the heat and sweat,
Where ice cream melts, a sticky threat.
Sunburned noses on parade,
As lemonade spills, a wild cascade.

Autumn whispers, leaves take flight,
While pumpkins dance in moon's soft light.
Each season sings a strange refrain,
Of laughter 'neath the sun and rain.

Spirits of the Shimmering Fields

In fields of gold, the sparklers play,
With twirling dances every day.
The wind tickles both grass and glee,
As spirits laugh in jubilee.

A scarecrow loves to tell a joke,
To corn stalks who silently choke.
His straw limbs flail, oh what a scene!
They giggle loud, an unseen team.

Fireflies blink, a disco game,
Lighting up the night, never the same.
With moves so slick, they steal the show,
In shimmering fields of gold aglow.

So if you wander through these plots,
Join the laughter, forget your thoughts.
For spirits roam, a cheeky crowd,
In shimmering fields, where joy is loud!

Whispers of the Forgotten Lands

In a meadow where the cows play,
A chicken clucks in dismay.
The gopher's juggling wild root,
While squirrels critique his suit.

Old trees gossip in a breeze,
About the time they climbed those leaves.
A rabbit's hop, a turtle's race,
They laugh and roll, oh what a place!

Dragonflies doing a cancan,
Blaming the wind, they can't withstand.
Toads are dancing with no beat,
As ants march on with tiny feet.

So if you wander, take a glance,
Nature's pulsing with a chance.
To find a tale, a giggle shared,
In lands where laughter's freely aired.

Chronicles Beneath the Sky

The clouds are all in a ruckus,
One's got a mustache—quite the fuss!
The sun throws shade, a playful jest,
While rainbows laugh, "We're the best!"

A wizard in flip-flops, casting spells,
With mismatched socks—that's how he dwells.
The stars got lost in a game of tag,
Chasing comets, a shootin' brag!

Balloons float over a picnic fair,
As ants compete to climb up air.
They carry crumbs, quite the burden,
While bees host raves—who would've certain?

So lift your gaze, and ponder why,
The universe loves a silly high.
In cosmic fun, we all can dive,
Under the laughs where dreams arrive!

Tides of the Ancient Echo

The ocean's hum like an old grandpa,
Sings tales of fish who go, "Ha, ha!"
Mermaids giggle with tails that twirl,
As seahorses play in a swirl.

A crab puts on a tiny shoe,
Declaring to shells, "I'm chic, who knew?"
The waves bring in a sandcastle crew,
Throwing a party, just for two!

Canvas of kelp, a floating scarf,
While dolphins whistle and bark like a larf.
A whale does a belly flop, oh my!
While gulls swoop down for a slice of pie.

So dive on in, among the cheer,
With every splash, let's shed a tear.
For life beneath the foamy crest,
Is filled with chuckles, and endless jest!

Legends of the Woven Roots

In a forest where trees wear crowns,
Rabbits gossip, exchanging frowns.
Leaves are daydreaming of tea-time,
While squirrels compose a forest rhyme.

The wise owl, with glasses on,
Reads tales from dusk to early dawn.
Foxes play poker with acorns bright,
Lowkey legends of a midnight fight!

Woodpeckers drum with a catchy beat,
As badgers bring snacks for a cozy seat.
A raccoon claims he's a knight on a quest,
While critters gather for a lively jest.

So stomp your feet, join the crew,
In tales of whimsy, all welcome you.
For in these roots, where giggles sprout,
Legends are woven, we laugh about!

Beneath the Gaze of Eternal Mountains

Mountains peek down, they wear a frown,
Wondering why we walk around.
We trip on rocks and tumble slow,
Their silent laughs, an echoing show.

A goat laughs loud, with horns so grand,
"You call that climbing? Please, let me stand!"
He leaps with grace, we grimace and flop,
Chasing our dreams, yet always we stop.

Clouds float by, with snickers so light,
They whisper tales of our awkward flight.
Oh, to defy gravity's tug,
Yet here we are, in a tangled rug.

At sunset's glow, we finally rest,
Mountains still chuckle, we did our best.
Under their gaze, we laugh and sing,
For in our fall, we found our spring.

The Chronicle of Echoing Crags

The crags shout back, when I call their name,
"Stop your noise! This isn't a game!"
But echoes bounce, with giggles and glee,
"Don't blame us, bud! It's just you and me!"

Each rocky face has stories to share,
Of lost wanderers and folks unaware.
I slip on a stone and sound like a drum,
Crags chuckle loud, 'Be careful, you bum!'

With every steep climb, I grumble and pout,
But the jagged rocks just can't live without,
Their humor displayed in ground-shaking fun,
Playing tricks on me 'til the day is done.

So here I stand, in their playful clutch,
Where laughter and safety never quite touch.
In echoing crags, my spirit soars,
For nothing beats joy that nature restores.

An Odyssey Through Whispering Woods

In the woods of whispers, trees start to tease,
"Don't stray too far, you might trip on bees!"
I stumble around, dodging branches that poke,
While bushes giggle, like they're part of the joke.

A squirrel takes flight with acorns in tow,
"Hey, where you going?" I yell, feeling low.
He scrambles up high, as if he can't hear,
While laughter echoes, trees cheer with good cheer.

A rustle, a flutter, what could it be?
A raccoon comes waltzing, so fancy, so free!
He tips his hat, "Do you dance with the breeze?"
As I trip on a root, he winks and just leaves.

At twilight's hour, the woods bow with grace,
We shared a dance, in this silly place.
Through whispers and giggles, my heart found a home,
In the land of the trees, I'm never alone.

The Firefly's Lantern

Fireflies glowing, they laugh in the night,
"Catch us if you can, it's quite a delight!"
With flickering lights, they lead me astray,
While I trip and slip, chasing dreams on display.

In rhythm they dance, a feisty parade,
"Oh human, come join us! We've made a charade!"
But I swing and sway, like a funky old tune,
As the fireflies giggle, 'We're not dancing soon!'

They twirl and they spin, with such charming flair,
While I puff and huff, gasping for air.
But in this lightshow, my heart starts to gleam,
For laughter and joy are the heart of the dream.

So here in the dark, I find my own light,
A firefly friend, in the soft summer night.
Together we glow, in a dance so divine,
As their joyous laughter becomes truly mine.

Threads of the Lost Canopy

In trees where squirrels lose their minds,
They plot their quests and draw funny signs.
A napkin map for hidden nuts,
While owls just hoot and laugh at such.

The branches sway like a great parade,
With acorns rolling, plans they made.
Hiding from the hawks up high,
They think they're stealthy—oh my, oh my!

A raindrop falls, a slip and slide,
The forest floor becomes their ride.
With giggles and grunts, they scurry around,
In a comical circus, nature's playground.

This canopy, a world of jest,
Nature's humor put to the test.
If only trees could laugh and sing,
They'd join in on the chaos—what fun it would bring!

Treasures of the Rooted Depths

Buried deep where the grubs all play,
The roots whisper tales in murky decay.
A goldfish's dream of being a king,
While clovers chuckle at a worm's bling.

Oh, treasures hidden, so weirdly placed,
Found by the beetles in a hurried race.
A shoe from a child, a bottle cap crown,
They grab shiny junk, feeling like a clown.

Underneath where the shadows creep,
Moles might host a wild, silly leap.
Digging for treasures, they face such strife—
They find an old spoon that once had a life.

Digging through dirt, what a delight,
These rooted wonders are their true height.
With laughter abiding in every bend,
Their earthbound antics have no end!

The Dance of the Endless Seasons

Spring tips-toes in, with flowers aglow,
While winter chuckles, just vibing below.
Summer's wild parties? Oh, what a view!
Fall's colorful dance is a riot, it's true!

Each season winks, as they play their parts,
Giggling blossoms with laughter in their hearts.
Winter throws snowballs, but all in good cheer,
While autumn flips leaves like they're out for a beer.

When springtime hops in, it's a wild affair,
With bunnies in bowties, what a sight to wear!
As summer's heat brings a sunburn with style,
They throw shade and swing, it's a giant guile!

The dance never ends, just spins round and round,
Seasons just laugh, as they play on this ground.
A cycle so silly, nature's own song,
Together they twirl, all the seasons belong!

Myths Born from the Dust

Once upon a time, in a mound of muck,
Lived creatures so silly, some thought it bad luck.
A tale of a snail who raced a fast hare,
And ended up stuck in a mossy old chair.

The dust held secrets of critters' delight,
A battle of wits, a comical fight.
Rabbits with tiaras, and bugs with their bling,
All sat around to see who could sing!

A creature proclaimed, "I found the best snack!"
But tripped on a twig and fell on its back.
The laughter exploded, a chorus so grand,
In the dirt where their fables took humorous stand.

So when you find stories in dust and in grime,
Remember these critters, and their sweet rhyme.
For myths are born from the quirks of the day,
In a world filled with laughter where silliness plays!

Whispers from the Depths of the Valley

In valleys low where shadows creep,
A squirrel swings, not missing sleep.
He wears a hat, quite out of style,
And cracks jokes in his own wild aisle.

A bouncing rabbit hops with glee,
He challenges a tree to a race, you see.
While frogs debate who needs a croak,
The gopher sneezes—what a joke!

The clouds above, they laugh and chuckle,
As ants form lines just for a cuddle.
The wind tells tales of clouds' great height,
While snails glide by, just taking flight.

With each odd critter, we find delight,
In nature's show, all day and night.
A valley's heart is where we play,
In laughter's grip, we'll always stay.

A Pilgrimage Across the Endless Horizon

On a quest to find the sunlit sass,
A turtle leads, he moves so fast!
He claims he'll beat the sunset's hue,
But naps instead, as turtles do.

A flock of birds sings songs of old,
While one stray chick asks, "Where's the gold?"
They search for treasures, oh so grand,
Just to find a piece of sand!

The horizon stretches wide and far,
With crazy dreams, like wishing stars.
A dancing cloud joins in the throng,
And asks the rhinos to sing along.

With jokes of grass and clouds that drift,
This journey feels like quite the gift.
Together they'll find joy and cheer,
While laughter echoes, never fear!

Nature's Silent Reverie

In quiet woods, the trees conspire,
To gossip low of fox and fire.
An owl who hoots a polka beat,
Is quite the star on woodland street.

While bushes bloom with silly names,
Like 'Tickle Me' and 'Silly Games'.
The flowers giggle as they sway,
With secret dreams of bright ballet.

A hedgehog writes with quill so fine,
His poetry's replete with pine.
A beetle taps; a soapstone drum,
While shadows scoot, they want some fun!

In reverie, the critters dance,
In every blink, a touch of chance.
The forest hums a merry tune,
As sunlight kisses afternoon.

In the Realm of Timeless Nights

Under stars that wink and shine,
A raccoon plots a heist divine.
He snatches snacks from bins with flair,
Then dances off without a care.

The moon's a big, bright laughing face,
As owls zoom by, they set the pace.
A secret party starts to bloom,
With twilight owls that burst with boom!

The fireflies join in leaps and bounds,
With luminous lights—joyic sounds.
They play hide-and-seek in sweet delight,
While crickets chirp to keep it tight.

In this realm, where time does freeze,
They share their tales with such great ease.
In giggling whispers, dreams take flight,
As critters revel through the night.

Heartbeats of the Evergreen

In the forest, trees do sway,
Squirrels dance and sing all day.
Branches whisper cheeky tales,
While mushrooms wear tiny veils.

Pinecones fall like little bombs,
Sending critters into qualms.
Birds cracking jokes, a real delight,
Nature's laughter in the night.

Beneath the boughs, shadows play,
Mice tell stories, won't delay.
Leaves are giggling in the breeze,
Barking dogs join in with ease.

So if you wander near and far,
Look for fun under the star.
In the woods, we find our glee,
Nature's jesters, wild and free.

Telling Tales Beneath a Canopy of Stars

Under stars, the stories twirl,
Fireflies dance, a glowing swirl.
Owls hoot puns on branches high,
As crickets chirp their lullaby.

A raccoon dons a chef's white hat,
Cooking up dreams and cheese for fat.
The moon rolls laughter in its glow,
While shadows giggle down below.

Every twinkle holds a joke so bright,
With the night as our stage, we delight.
Ghosts of legends take a dive,
Making sure we feel alive.

So gather round, let stories flow,
Beneath the stars, let chuckles grow.
For in this space where dreams align,
Laughter's the drink, oh how divine!

The Threads of Nature's Song

With threads of green and hues of gold,
Nature weaves tales, bold and old.
A caterpillar's ticklish crawl,
Sends giggles up from plants so tall.

Butterflies wear gowns with flair,
While bees buzz in their fine hair.
The river laughs a bubbly tune,
As frogs perform beneath the moon.

Squirrels plot with acorns galore,
Scavenging not a second more.
Each leaf a note in the grand score,
Nature's orchestra we adore.

So join the dance, let laughter bloom,
In green pastures, shake off the gloom.
For every song has a lighter tone,
In nature's arms, we find a home.

Solace Beneath the Weeping Willow

Weeping willow, what tales you tell,
Of ants who march and crickets quell.
Beneath your branches, secrets lie,
Where butterflies sip tea and sigh.

A rabbit hops, with velvet ears,
Counting laughs instead of fears.
And twirling leaves, a merry sight,
Spin stories woven with pure delight.

In your shade, the world feels bright,
As dandelions take to flight.
Here, we laugh at the softest breeze,
Hearing jokes whispered from the trees.

Oh, willow dear, hold us close,
In your comfort, we find the most.
For laughter lingers in your grace,
We find our joy, a warm embrace.

In the Odyssey of Still Waters

In a boat made of marshmallows, they set out,
With a crew of ducks, that quacked about.
They paddled with spoons, not oars in sight,
Chasing shiny fish that flickered with light.

A sea of jellybeans, waves of cream,
They sailed through a daydream, a sweet little scheme.
Each splash brought laughter, a giggle or two,
As they tried to catch clouds, just for a view.

But the ducks had their plans, they wanted to snack,
Turning the boat into a quacky attack.
With bill-full of snack cakes, the journey was slow,
As they feasted on treats, their giggles would grow.

They reached the still waters, stars in their eyes,
There stood a marshmallow castle in the skies.
With laughter and cheer, they danced on the shore,
In the odyssey of giggles, who could want more?

The Keeper of Forgotten Legends

In a library where books wear tiny crowns,
Lived a keeper who'd tell tales of silly clowns.
He spoke of the heroes, the ones who could dance,
Who battled with donuts and took their chance.

A dragon with hiccups, on a quest for a cake,
Tried blowing out candles, but only caused wake.
The townsfolk all laughed, as he sneezed out a pie,
As cookies rained down from the sweetened sky.

With treasure maps drawn on a pancake plate,
They found hidden syrup, oh what a fate!
They fought jelly monsters with spoons at the ready,
In this epic of giggles, their laughs kept steady.

The tales were absurd, but oh so much fun,
A kingdom of legends, where laughter's the sun.
So come sit with the keeper, and hear all the tales,
Of giggly adventures and syrup-filled sails!

A Saga Written in Moonlight

Underneath the moon, with its big silly grin,
A goat wearing spectacles, began to spin.
He spun and he twirled, on a stage made of cheese,
As mice held their breath, hoping he'd please.

With jokes made of crickets and laughter of frogs,
He juggled with fireflies, like colorful logs.
Each flicker a chuckle, igniting the night,
While the stars all cheered, what a glorious sight!

The audience roared, for a tuba made noise,
And danced with the rhythm, those silly old boys.
But the moon just sighed, "I've seen better sights,"
As it hummed to the tune of the happy delights.

At dawn, our goat stumbled, tumbling in glee,
With dreams of new antics, oh what could they be?
In the saga of moonlight, filled with laughter and cheer,
The night came alive, as it drank up the beer!

The Language of Distant Thunder

When thunder began as a big belly laugh,
The clouds rolled in, on their silly behalf.
They tickled the trees and danced on the ground,
Singing songs of joy in a booming sound.

With lightning like sparkles on a birthday cake,
The world felt more vibrant, it started to shake.
Raindrops became giggles, a shower of fun,
As puddles reflected the light of the sun.

The squirrels held meetings, plotting their raids,
They debated on acorns, with mighty charades.
A ruckus erupted, with a flip and a flap,
As thunder boomed louder, they danced in a hap.

In the distance, the laughter rang crystal and clear,
With echoes of joy that tickled the ear.
Language of thunder, a comedy's prize,
Bringing smiles to the world, beneath stormy skies.

Legends in the Misty Glade

In the glade where mushrooms dance,
A squirrel tried to win a prance.
He tripped on roots and made a splash,
But still he smiled, that little rascal.

A frog recited tales of cheer,
While birds just chirped, 'We can't hear!'
A band of ants joined in the fest,
Claiming they were simply the best.

A breeze would blow, the leaves would cheer,
As laughter echoed through the sphere.
With every tale, the laughter grew,
In this lush land, joy's never through.

So raise your cup of acorn juice,
And toast to friends, let's turn it loose.
The misty glade holds stories bright,
Of funny mishaps and pure delight.

The Guardians of the Verdant Realm

In the realm where the green leaves sway,
Guardians gather, come what may.
A rabbit armed with a tiny shield,
Prepared to defend his leafy field.

An owl in glasses, wise and bold,
Told tales of brave, both young and old.
While hedgehogs rolled, a roly-poly crew,
Declaring that they were knights too!

With mushrooms crafted into hats,
And carrots sharp like polished bats.
These guardians fought with laughs, not strife,
Defending their patch, full of life.

And when the sun began to set,
They shared the stories they won't forget.
With merry hearts, they'd tell the tale,
Of how they conquered each blobby snail!

Testaments of the Celestial Firmament

Beneath a sky of twinkling stars,
The creatures pondered life's bizarre.
A hedgehog checked his horoscope,
While dreaming of a far-off slope.

A bear proclaimed he'd soar so high,
If only he could learn to fly.
He flapped his arms and gave a grin,
And tumbled down, took it on the chin.

The raccoons sold maps to the moon,
Claiming a ride would come up soon.
But all they found were tipsy bees,
Performing dances on the breeze.

With giggles ringing through the night,
They shared their tales, a playful sight.
In this vast space, where dreams do bloom,
The firmament echoed with laughter's plume.

The Call of the Sturdy Hills

On sturdy hills where whispers roam,
The gnomes decided to make a home.
With beards so long and hats so tall,
They fashioned houses, one and all.

A goat came by with a cheeky grin,
Claiming he could out-dance them, win.
But tangled horns in a prancing feat,
Left him hopping on his tiny feet.

The wind would chuckle through the grass,
As stories floated, none would pass.
With clinks and clanks, they shared their brews,
In warm camaraderie, it infused.

So heed the call, join in the thrill,
On sturdy hills, life's never still.
With laughter echoing all around,
In each small corner, joy is found.

Fables from the Falling Rain.

Once a snail, in wartime gear,
Said, "I'm ready, have no fear!"
He challenged frogs to leap and croak,
But lost the race—what a joke!

Clouds rumbled, thunder let loose,
The snail slipped and had to choose:
To hide in shell or to be bold—
He took a nap, dreams uncontrolled!

Raindrops fell like playful sprites,
While puddles danced in silly fights.
With each splash, a story found,
Of snails and frogs, all merry sounds!

So next time when it starts to pour,
Remember snails who dream of lore.
For in the rain, there lies a tale—
Of goofy races, rainy gales!

Whispers of Forgotten Valleys

In valleys deep where whispers play,
Lived goats who wore a wig each day.
They strutted, pranced, with flair so fine,
Each thought themselves a star divine.

One day they had a dance-off brave,
But all they did was trip and wave.
With twirls that spun and legs that flew,
The goats were graced—by mud, not dew!

Behind the rocks, a squirrel laughed,
And then began to draft a draft.
A book of goat-fails, quite a hit,
For valley tales, it sure was lit!

So if you roam where whispers hide,
Watch for goats, in sequins they glide.
For laughter blooms in valleys wide,
With goats that dance, and pride beside!

Into the Heart of Ancient Forests

In ancient woods, the trees would chat,
One shared a tale of a sneaky cat.
He climbed so high to catch a bird,
But instead fell—oh, how absurd!

The birds exclaimed, "What a sight to see!"
As branches shook in wild decree.
With leaves a-titter, they danced around,
While the plucky cat fell, safe and sound.

A wise old owl in glasses perched,
Said, "Cats and trees should not be searched!"
He scribbled notes, a guide to feasts,
For forest folks and furry beasts.

So if you wander where trees conspire,
Look for cats—both brave and dire.
Laughter echoes through the leaves,
In forests where imagination weaves!

The Last Echo of the Wild

In jungle green, the monkeys screeched,
They claimed the title of king, all reached.
They declared it a royal patch,
But fell from trees—oh, what a match!

The parrots cawed a witty jest,
Saying, "Monkeys, stick to your quest!"
With laughter loud, they swung about,
And showed that glee is what it's about.

Beneath the canopy, shadows play,
While critters dance in the light of day.
The wild remembers those who care,
And echoes joy, floating in air.

So join the jest, in nature's might,
For every twist brings a new delight.
With echoes ringing through the trees,
The wild is filled with giggles and ease!

The Palette of Dawn's Awakening

In the morning light, colors clash,
A rooster near the fence makes a splash.
He crows like he's the king of the lot,
While sleepy cats plot their next big plot.

Brushstrokes of orange, pink, and gray,
The sun flips on its lights in a playful way.
Squirrels in suits debate on the lawn,
While daisies giggle as the dewdrops yawn.

Clouds dress up, parade in the sky,
A butterfly winks, oh me, oh my!
The world spins like a top, wild and free,
In colors so bright, who can disagree?

As daylight unfolds, the scene's set bright,
With whispers of dreams laughing in flight.
Coffee brews, a symphony of scents,
Drawing us in, each moment it rents.

Windblown Stories of Forgotten Trails

Along the path where the daisies grow,
The wind tells yarns, both high and low.
A tumbleweed winks, it's seen it all,
From cowboys' tales to the wild owl's call.

Leaves dance in circles, doing a jig,
While acorns strategize, feeling quite big.
The old oak chuckles, still standing proud,
As squirrels rehearse their acorn crowd.

Over hills so green, the breezes weave,
Of mischief and laughter, on this eve.
Each twist and turn a story to share,
With wind as the bard, light as the air.

Golden sunsets blush, the day tilts away,
Whispering secrets of the playful fray.
Underneath the stars, the stories will soar,
As moonlight giggles, asking for more.

When the Rivers Speak

Listen closely, the rivers hum,
With tales of fish that dance and run.
A grumpy old turtle grumbles with glee,
While minnows giggle, "Come dance with me!"

Raging rapids roar like a loud fool,
As frogs in tuxedos form a pool school.
Whispers of pebbles share secrets old,
While otters slide by, bold and cold.

The moon dips low, and the waters glow,
Fishes gossip, making big show.
Underwater parties, it's quite a sight,
With bubbles and splashes, they party all night.

When the rivers chat, you'll shake with glee,
With laughter that ripples as wild as can be.
A world aquatic, oh what a spree,
When currents collide and hearts run free!

The Dance of Time Among the Stones

Time twirls on rocks like a playful sprite,
With shadows that stretch, oh what a sight!
Pebbles gossip, each a grand sage,
While history's waltz fills the stage.

Ancient stones grin as dancers glide,
While clocks tick loudly, but none can hide.
Hiccups of laughter skip with each beat,
As time pirouettes, feeling quite fleet.

Rusty old signs chuckle, pointing the way,
"To cliffs and to valleys, let's dance every day!"
The grass joins in with a sway and a shake,
With whispers of ages that none can fake.

As stars roll in and the moon takes a glance,
Time spins in circles in a merry dance.
With rocks as the chorus, the night may just gleam,
In the joyous ballet of every sweet dream.

The Wind's Lament in Silent Valleys

The breeze grumbles low in the hills,
Whispering tales of peculiar spills.
With gales that giggle and gusts that tease,
It tickles the trees with the greatest of ease.

It swirls round stones with a whooshing sound,
As if searching for jokes hidden underground.
The flowers all chuckle, they sway with delight,
While clouds roll their eyes at this comical fright.

Yet in quiet moments, it sighs and it moans,
Complaining of leaves that can't find their homes.
The poor winds are playful, just longing for fun,
But valleys stay silent, their laughter's on the run.

So the Wind yields its punchlines, a bit out of breath,
Telling tall tales of the valley's own death.
With a wink and a twist, it takes off to the skies,
Leaving behind chuckles that never say goodbye.

Guardians of the Hidden Grove

There's a tribe of squirrels in the woods so lush,
Dressed in cool cloaks of the softest blush.
They guard acorns fiercely, with utmost pride,
While raccoons sneak in for a snack on the side.

The owls hoot nonsense from their lofty perches,
Reciting old riddles and causing new searches.
Each night's a debate with who's wisdom the best,
But laughter erupts, it's a raucous jest.

The trees kindly shake, as they chuckle along,
While crickets provide the most whimsical song.
They dance under stars that are winking in time,
In a spectacle bursting with nature's own rhyme.

When moonlight peeks through with a glimmering beam,
Guardians giggle softly, in whimsical dream.
As the night fades away with the dawn's gentle rise,
The secrets of nature share looks full of ties.

Reverie of the Mountain Spirits

High up where echoes craft stories anew,
The spirits convene, with a raucous crew.
They tumble like snowflakes, with laughter so grand,
Creating a symphony across the wide land.

While boulders are bopping to melodies low,
They gossip of valleys and rivers that flow.
Each brush of the wind sends them reeling in glee,
As shadows of mountains join in their spree.

With giggles as fresh as a crisp mountain stream,
They ponder on woolly clouds' thoughts and dreams.
Jokes about glaciers that sneak up with grace,
Are met with a chuckle, a playful embrace.

As dusk paints the peaks with a brush dipped in gold,
The spirits are giddy, sharing stories untold.
A mountain's wild laughter rings out through the mist,
With a wink and a nod, oh, you can't let it twist!

The Sigh of Enduring Landscapes

The hills rumble softly with a contented sigh,
As if all of nature cracked jokes in the sky.
Rivers ripple laughter, trickling down fast,
While valleys retain all the secrets they cast.

The rocks wear a grin, so rugged and wise,
While meadows engage in their best butterfly flies.
With flowers in bloom and buds trying to peek,
The scenery hosts its own comedic streak.

When rain showers tumble with mischievous glee,
They splash on the canvas of the greenery.
While sunbeams giggle as they peek through the haze,
The earth dances merrily in warm hazy rays.

Yet as sunsets paint purple and orange so bright,
The landscapes unite in one final delight.
They chuckle and chuckle at everything near,
In harmony singing, "Now isn't this queer?"

Beneath the Watchful Pines

Beneath the pines, a squirrel danced,
With acorns flying, he pranced and pranced.
A raccoon chuckled from a nearby tree,
"You think you're quick? Just wait and see!"

The pines were swaying, a rhythm so grand,
While birds were singing in a quirky band.
The forest echoed with laughter so bright,
As the critters partied deep into the night.

A fox in a hat joined the fun with flair,
Claiming his moves had style to spare.
The owl rolled his eyes, with wisdom unmatched,
Said, "It's just a dance, who cares if you're hatched?"

So beneath those pines, the tales rolled on,
Of goofy gnomes and a jester's brawn.
Nature's sitcom, a scene to behold,
Where joy is eternal, and never grows old.

Echoes of the Enchanted Glade

In a glade of whispers, a frog wore a crown,
While rabbits debated who really ran town.
"I leap with prowess!" the frog proudly croaked,
But the bunnies just giggled, and one softly joked.

The fairies all fluttered, their lights all aglow,
As they painted the night with a shimmering show.
A gnome stole some glitter, proclaiming with zest,
"This disco ball's mine! I'm the life of the fest!"

Amidst all the laughter, a tree stump held sway,
Where sip of hot cocoa led to wild play.
They roared with amusement, as shadows would sway,
In the glade where the magic refused to decay.

So remember this glade, where giggles take flight,
A land full of joy, in the soft, silver light.
Where every old stump and each leaf on the breeze,
Is filled with a whimsy that aims to please.

The Moon's Caress on Frosted Fields

On frosted fields, the moon did prance,
With a wink and a nod, in a shimmering dance.
The owls wore tuxedos, looking quite grand,
While a mouse in a bow tie asked, "Want to dance?"

The frost made it slippery, a sight to see,
As they twirled and stumbled, oh how they'd flee!
The stars were all laughing, twinkling in glee,
As the critters made legends of snowy jubilee.

A hedgehog in skates tried to glide with flair,
But collided with bushes, oh what a scare!
The bunnies just rolled, their giggles a tide,
In a frosty pandemonium, nobody would hide.

In the glow of the moon and the chilly night air,
The creatures of winter shed all their cares.
So if you find laughter on those frosted hills,
Join in the fun, and enjoy the thrills!

Chronicles of Forgotten Legacies

In tales of yore, the turtles would boast,
Of forgotten legacies, they loved the most.
They spoke of the days when they raced with pride,
But now just lay still, let the sun be their guide.

A snail recounted the legends so grand,
Of a race he once lost to a swift, crafty hand.
"I wasn't slow, just favoring dreams!"
He claimed to the crowd, with his whimsical schemes.

The bumblebees buzzed, sharing stories of woe,
Of flowers long gone, and the juice, oh so low!
"In times of great pollen, we danced with delight,
But now we just bumble from morning till night!"

So listen, dear friend, to the whispers of age,
In chronicles old, we each play a stage.
For laughter's the thread that weaves us as one,
In tales of our lives, where the humor won.

Songs of the Grounded Spirits

In the garden, gnomes all dance,
With tiny hats, they take their chance.
They jig and jig until they fall,
Plotting pranks at the fence wall.

Worms are whispering gossip loud,
While ants parade, feeling proud.
A tiny beetle, dressed in style,
Keeps strutting by with a big smile.

Bunnies hop in a grand ballet,
While flowers laugh, come join the play!
The sun winks down with a cheeky grin,
As nature chuckles, let the fun begin.

The mighty oak rolls its wise eye,
As squirrels hurl acorns on the fly.
It's a laugh riot beneath the trees,
Where mischief rides on the gentle breeze.

Shadows of the Unearthed Past

Buried treasures of silly lore,
With pirate caps and treasures galore!
Stumbling specters in playful fright,
Dance with dust in the moon's bright light.

Old bones giggle, as tales unfold,
Of adventures shared, both brave and bold.
Mummies wrapped in tattered pride,
Do the twist, ooh, side to side!

A phantom's hiccup echoes near,
While jesters joke with ghostly cheer.
Each shadow laughs with a timeless glee,
As long-lost spirits take a spree.

The graveyard's alive with their silly game,
Chasing echoes, who's to blame?
And in the dusk, their laughter rings,
In the homes of forgotten kings.

Horizons of the Uncharted Soil

Digging deep for hidden charms,
Moles are plotting their little harms.
Lively dirt with a twinkle bright,
Dares us all to take a bite!

In fields unknown, a treasure map,
Crickets chirp, "Come take a nap!"
Grasshoppers leap with a boisterous cheer,
All the groundlings want to steer clear.

Mud pies fly in a feast unplanned,
While pickles smile, oh isn't it grand?
Tomato fights, they all agree,
Nature's jest is the best decree!

So we'll gather, with giggles galore,
Finding treasures in dirt and more.
Soil so rich, it's a quirky delight,
Where laughter sprinkles in the night.

Voices in the Wind-Blown Fields

In the breezy plains, laughter sways,
Whispering secrets in playful ways.
A dandelion floats, grinning wide,
Says to the grass, "Let's go for a ride!"

Clouds are chuckling, with shapes so strange,
Making bunnies and fish in a range.
While chicory winks and twirls around,
Swaying gently to the silly sound.

A tumbleweed rolls in a wobbly dance,
Sharing stories of wild romance.
While sunflowers nod in a jovial spree,
Swaying their heads with glee, oh wee!

So we find joy in the open air,
With voices of nature, light as a prayer.
In fields where giggles and whispers play,
Join the ruckus, let's laugh all day!

Chronicles of the Distant Horizon

Upon a hill, a goat does dance,
A dragon's flight? Just a chance!
With wings made of cardboard and dreams,
It twirls and spins, or so it seems.

The clouds are sheep, fluffy and white,
Baa-ing along, oh what a sight!
An eagle wearing glasses so grand,
Read the news from the great beyond land.

A talking tree shares gossip so prime,
While squirrels debate the best wintertime!
With acorns for cash, they buy up the sun,
Chasing their futures, just a bit of fun!

The horizon chuckles, it seems to conspire,
With every giggle, it lifts us higher.
So here we stand, on this merry ground,
Listening closely, joy to be found.

The Gathering of the Rustling Leaves

Leaves gather 'round for a picnic so bright,
Discussing the best way to catch sunlight.
One leaf remarks, 'I'm just a proud sprout,'
While others argue what 'green' is about.

A gust of wind breaks into the fun,
Throws everyone's plans on the run!
'Chill out!' they shout, 'Let's just play tag!'
As they whirl and twirl in a colorful rag.

A chipmunk arrives, with stories to tell,
Of acorn-hoarding and seasons so swell.
They laugh and they boast about the best trees,
As the sun dips low and the shadows tease.

So here's to the leaves in a grand ole cheer,
Who thrive on giggles and have no fear.
Life's all a rustle, a twist, and a dance,
In twilight's embrace, they find a chance.

Requiem for the Untold Trails

A path unraveled, secrets it sways,
Covered in laughter, and doggy delays.
The squirrels all hoodie, wearing their threads,
Sharing their snacks and rebellious spreads.

A shoe left behind tells tales of great glee,
Of a prancing pup who just wouldn't agree.
With sticks for swords, they conquer the wild,
In this epic saga, they're all just a child.

Hens pecking whispers behind the tall grass,
Trading their gossip as seconds do pass.
A frog croaks out, "Then I leaped over that!"
While a raccoon rolls his eyes at the spat.

So tread lightly, friend, on these lively tracks,
For every step hides a giggle that cracks.
The untold trails call with humor so keen,
In the tale of the wild, you're the unwritten scene.

Fireside Stories of the Boundless Plains

Gather 'round, let's share a good tale,
Of a bear who wanted to ride a grey whale.
With popcorn and dreams beneath twinkling stars,
We'll laugh till our bellies round like those jars.

An owl with glasses read fortunes anew,
Said "You'll dance with the moon, just shake your shoe!"

A rabbit exclaimed, "But I'm late for my date!"
As everyone giggles, "You're just sort of great!"

The flames crackle stories of buns that were baked,
And the raccoon who claimed he could dance without quake.
With sparks in the air, his moves make us roar,
'Til a firefly yelled, "Please, not that encore!"

So let's toast marshmallows and share our own lore,
Of quirky mishaps and laughter galore.
In the boundless plains, where the silly run free,
Tell me your stories, come dance by with me!

Resonance of Timeworn Trails

Once I chased a silly hare,
He wore a hat and seemed so rare.
We dashed through woods with glee,
But he laughed and left me be.

My shoes were old, they squeaked with pride,
I tripped on roots and tried to hide.
The trees, they chuckled loud and clear,
As branches waved and drew me near.

A raccoon joined, with mischief planned,
Together we would take a stand.
Against the squirrels, oh what a sight,
We'd duel till day turned into night.

In shadows deep, we danced with glee,
A parade of oddities, just me.
The trails of old can't hold us tight,
For laughter leads us on our flight.

An Ode to the Sunlit Stones

Oh sunlit stones, you warm my sole,
You giggle as I take a stroll.
With every step, a crackling sound,
Like popcorn popped beneath the ground.

Some sit as pets beneath the sky,
And wink at clouds that drift on by.
They tell me tales of ancient times,
With boulders dropping punchline rhymes.

A rock informed me of a fight,
Between a snail and worm one night.
The snail declared, 'I'm shell-ious, see!'
The worm just sighed, 'You can't catch me!'

So there they squabbled, slow yet fast,
While sunlit stones watched and laughed.
An epic jest this world unfolds,
With quirky gems and stones of gold.

Secrets of the Wandering Rivers

Oh wandering rivers, what do you know?
You twist and turn, putting on a show.
With secrets wrapped in bubbles bright,
You giggle, splish, and splash with delight.

The fish are gossiping, having a ball,
'The catfish said this, the bass said that' call.
They mock my boat with fishy grins,
As I row on by with my tin can fins.

A turtle passing, slow as can be,
Said, 'Life's a race, but you'll never see!'
While frogs croak tunes of ancient lore,
Promising stories by the rivershore.

So I sit back, take a sip of tea,
And let the river carry me free.
Its twists and turns, a joyful spree,
With chuckles hidden in every decree.

Legends Carved in Autumn Leaves

In autumn's glow, the leaves take flight,
They dance and twirl, oh what a sight!
Each crispy crunch tells tales of yore,
Of squirrels that dare to dream and soar.

A maple leaf, with flair and grace,
Did pirouettes in an acorn race.
While oaks applauded, roots tapped in glee,
'Join us for tea, we're wild and free!'

The aspen chimed in, a fluttering muse,
It whispered secrets, tales to peruse.
Of heroes and legends, it stretched for fun,
'The forest's alive, just look, isn't it fun?'

As winds wove stories through branches high,
The leaves erupted with raucous sighs.
A symphony played in nature's grand weave,
Celebrating the joy that all can believe.

Ballads of the Waking Woods

In the woods where the squirrels chatter,
A raccoon sings, and it makes me splatter.
He steals my snack, I've lost my pie,
Blame it on the critter, oh my, oh my!

The trees wear hats of fluffy moss,
While rabbits hop, and they never pause.
Gather 'round, let the stories flow,
Of woodland parties held long ago.

A bear tried to dance, but stepped on a log,
He twirled too fast, now he's stuck like a frog.
The owls hoot laughter, deep in the night,
As stars above giggle in soft twilight.

With every rustle of leaves and glee,
The forest whispers its own jubilee.
Nature's own jesters, at play with you,
Come join the fun, we'll sing till we're through!

Journey Through the Stone-Crowned Valleys

In valleys deep where the stones do grin,
A goat went walking, he tripped, and fell in.
He popped up high, in a cloud of dust,
And then danced around like it was a must.

The rocks chuckle softly, they know the score,
While thistles giggle and shake to the core.
A lizard slides down, with a wink and a flip,
"Oh, come join in! Let's take a trip!"

With echoes that play in the winding trails,
We laugh at the creatures, each story prevails.
A snail took a cruise, oh what a sight,
As he sped past the boulders, declaring, "I'm light!"

The sun set low, with its golden rays,
The valleys erupted in joyful plays.
Each stone has a tale, a silly old joke,
Sing with the shadows 'til daylight awoke!

Murmurs of the Timeworn Earth

Oh, the dirt has tales that it loves to share,
Of worms with hats, and bugs with flair.
They argue who's king of the underground,
With giggles and grumbles, laughter abound.

The trees gossip, their branches entwined,
About a round rock that's surprisingly kind.
He tells all the seeds they can grow up grand,
In a world full of giggles, it's all so unplanned.

A fox in a cloak took a stroll at dusk,
Slipped on a root, made a big, funny fuss.
The moon watched closely, holding her breath,
As nature's own jesters jumped with zest!

With whispers of magic on each little path,
The earth keeps on giggling, sharing its laughs.
Step lightly, dear friend, in this jolly place,
For laughter and joy are a grand embrace!

The Symphony of Weathered Footprints

Footprints dance upon the sandy shore,
Each tells a tale of adventures galore.
A crab in a tuxedo, quite the display,
Waves to the crowd, "Come join my ballet!"

The gulls squawk a tune that's oddly domestic,
While starfish applaud, their arms quite eclectic.
A jellyfish giggles, swirling in glee,
"If I could wear shoes, they'd be fancy like me!"

Children run wild, chasing shadows that flee,
While seaweed applauds with a whimsical glee.
A wave comes to play, then sneezes in mirth,
"Oh, bless me! I'm tickled by this crazy earth!"

The sun sets in colors, a magical sight,
As footprints blur, twinkling with delight.
The shoreline whispers, "Join in the fun,
For every step taken is joy, not just done!"

Journey Through the Realm of Shadows

In the land where shadows prance,
A fearless mouse sought his chance.
He wore a hat far too large,
And swayed like a tiny barge.

With every step, he tripped and spun,
Avoiding rocks just for fun.
His friends rolled eyes, then laughed out loud,
As he danced around, a silly crowd.

A ghostly cat joined in the dance,
Hoping for a second chance.
But it turned out to be a trap,
Leading him to a nap.

So shadows laugh while day turns night,
In their realm, there's pure delight.
With every blunder, joy does unfold,
In this tale, brave and bold.

In the Embrace of Ancient Oaks

Beneath the boughs of oaks so wise,
A squirrel plots with gleamy eyes.
He hoards acorns, thinks he's sly,
But forgets where he dumped them, oh my!

A raccoon joins, with dreams of gold,
Whispers of treasures from ages old.
But all they find in the leafy maze,
Are socks and shoes from former days.

The oak said nothing, just swayed and creaked,
While the friends giggled, slightly freaked.
In the presence of giants, moments seem light,
Even lost socks can spark pure delight.

As day fades, with laughter so thick,
They toast with acorns, a cheeky trick.
In the arms of nature, they find their glee,
In ancient oaks, wild and free.

The Silent Watcher of the Starlit Lake

By the lake, where stars reflect,
A frog planned mischief, what the heck!
With a crown made of lily pads,
He dreamed of ruling all the lads.

A fish rolled by, in quite a stir,
Wondering why the frog's a blur.
"Your crown's not real," it voiced with glee,
"Just fluff from the plant and some debris!"

The frog took pride, with a little wink,
"Beauty is all in how you think!"
The fish, amused, declared a jest:
"In your kingdom, I'm still the best!"

Tonight, they sit under twinkling skies,
With silly crowns and dreaming eyes.
For in this world where absurdities wake,
Laughter flows from the starlit lake.

An Invitation to the Timeless Journey

A snail with dreams of speed and grace,
Set out one day, with a cheerful face.
"I'll roam the world," he called so loud,
While ants lined up, a curious crowd.

They offered rides on a sturdy leaf,
For snails like him, beyond belief.
"Hop on back, we'll race the night!"
But they just giggled, oh what a sight!

The journey began, with foods galore,
With pizza crumbs and chocolate, what a score!
Though no one rushed, they had their bids,
And laughed at plans that life always skids.

So time went by, in playful bliss,
With journeys shared, bigger than this.
Together they traveled, little and grand,
In a whimsical world, hand in hand.

Songs of the Unsung Tempest

In the stormy skies, a chicken clucks,
Wings flapping wildly, not giving up.
The clouds roll in, the winds do sway,
As thunder rolls, the critters play.

Raindrops fall like jelly beans,
Splashing puddles, oh what scenes!
A dancing frog, a funny sight,
In muddy boots, they leap with delight.

The lightning strikes, a flash, a pop,
The goat next door just won't stop!
With a horned head and a silly grin,
He's the bravest in the wind's loud din.

So raise a toast to weather gone wild,
To the tempest's pranks, like a mischief child.
For every gust, a laugh we'll share,
In the chaos, fun is everywhere!

The Whispering Meadow's Promise

In fields of grass where daisies bloom,
A sneaky mouse plots in the gloom.
He dreams of cheese, oh what a feat,
But tumbles down, oh how discreet!

Butterflies flutter, having a feast,
While ants march on, never to cease.
A ladybug winks, oh what a tease,
As they hide behind tall, swaying trees.

Crickets chirp the evening's tune,
While frogs join in, singing soon.
A party starts under the moon's glow,
With all the critters putting on a show.

And when the stars twinkle bright,
The meadow laughs with sheer delight.
For every whisper that the grass knows,
Is a giggle shared with every rose.

A Tapestry Woven in Twilight

In twilight's grip, the stars take stage,
While owls debate in wise old rage.
A moth flutters, thinking he's bright,
But the porch light giggles at his plight.

Bats weave through strands of the evening air,
Chasing shadows with debonair flair.
A rabbit hops, wearing a hat,
As if it's fancy, oh imagine that!

Fireflies blink in a dance so spry,
While crickets serenade with a soft sigh.
The trees eavesdrop, leaning in close,
To listen to secrets that none would expose.

So here's to twilight, with its chaotically glee,
A tapestry woven, spirited and free.
For every mishap under the fading sun,
Is a hilarious tale, a laugh to be spun.

The Last Flight of the Soaring Eagle

Upon a cliff, an eagle waits,
His feathered friend on chance creates.
With a mighty flap, he takes to flight,
But lands like a rock, oh what a sight!

A hairpin turn, a gust of wind,
He soars and doubt he must rescind.
Yet upside down, he gleefully spins,
Winging it well, but not for wins.

On the ground, a crowd does cheer,
For every tumble, they hold dear.
An acorn drops, he gives a shout,
And gathers friends for a little bout.

So here's to the eagle, who dreams so high,
With laughter echoing across the sky.
For every failed flight, there's a tale untold,
Of friendship, spirit, and bravery bold.

www.ingramcontent.com/pod-product-compliance
Lightning Source LLC
Chambersburg PA
CBHW072130070526
44585CB00016B/1615